America's
ROBERT E. LEE

Henry Steele
Commager

&

Lynd Ward

HOUGHTON MIFFLIN
COMPANY BOSTON

To NELLIE THOMAS McCOLL

It was something to be born a Lee, in Virginia. All through the South there were great families that dominated society — and politics and war too — but nowhere was there a greater or a prouder family than the Lee. For over a hundred years the Lees played a leading part in the history of the Old Dominion. They had been Governors and Councillors and Burgesses. They had served the King, had fought in the Revolution, sat in the Continental Congress, and represented their country

at foreign courts. They had been great planters, great states-
men, great soldiers. Two Lees had written their names on
the Declaration of Independence, under the flourishing signa-
ture of John Hancock — but Lees needed no flourish to their
names! "I know of no country that can produce a family all
distinguished as clever men, as our Lees," said Washington,
who knew them well.

A sort of Lee cousinship spread like a network over the whole
state. Little Robert Edward didn't know it yet, but he was
cousin to the Carters and the Randolphs, the Tazewells and
the Peytons, the Blands and the Corbins, the Fitzhughs and
the Nicholases and a dozen others. And there wasn't a great
plantation in the whole Tidewater where the Lees weren't
welcome.

He had been born in mid-winter of 1807, at Stratford, in
the same room in which two signers of the Declaration of
Independence had been born. What a wonderful place Stratford was — a great brick house, sitting low on the land, with
massive walls four feet thick, with two immense chimneys,
larger than any others to be found in the whole of America,
and with a promenade on the roof from which you could see
the broad shining Potomac River. There was an elegant
ballroom, the handsomest, it was said, in all Virginia, and
each of the other rooms — there were seventeen in all — was
painted a different color. There was a blue room and a white
room, a green room and a cherry room, and each with a fireplace big enough to hide in. From the walls hung portraits
of ancestors frowning down, or smiling, as they chose, in their
stiff, formal clothes and their powdered wigs.

And Stratford was more than a house; it was a whole village,
with cook houses and an office and a schoolroom, and stables
all close to the big house, and the Negro quarters off at a distance,
but not too far for adventure. Best of all for a boy were the
acres and acres of land, shaded by great poplars and oaks and

sugar maples and cedars. A little way off was shallow Pope's Creek to wade in, and the Potomac with the great sailing boats going up and down.

He was the third boy, and was named Robert Edward, after his mother's brothers. She was a Carter, and if there was any family in Virginia that could hold its own with the Lees, it was the Carters. Grandfather Charles Carter — himself son of a planter so rich and splendid that he had been called "King" Carter — lived at Shirley on the James River, and during his boyhood Robert spent more time at Shirley than at Stratford. Shirley was almost as famous as Stratford, and even more elegant: people came from far and wide to see the wonderful staircase that seemed to hang suspended in the air, and to see the painting of General Washington by the Philadelphia artist, Charles Peale, that hung so proudly in the drawing room. The Carter clan was even more wide-flung than the Lee:

6

grandfather Carter had had no less than twenty-one children, and most of them had large families in turn, so wherever you went visiting in Virginia you ran into a Carter cousin — at Ravenswood and at Chatham and at Nomini Hall and Roswell, and so many others you could scarcely remember them all.

Yes, it was something to be born a Lee and to have a Carter mother. But it was hard to be a poor relation. Robert's father was the famous "Light-Horse Harry." He had been a hero in the Revolution, and Governor of Virginia and General Washington admired him. But Light-Horse Harry's career was all in the past — and his fame and fortune too. He would still ride off at the head of the little army that put down the so-called "Whiskey Rebellion"; he would still serve in Congress, and propose the famous resolution to Washington — "first in war, first in peace, and first in the hearts of his countrymen." But, after all the glamor of the Revolution and the Governor-

ship, Light-Horse Harry found it hard to settle down to the humdrum life of a planter. He just wasn't meant for the quiet life. Soon he owed money, lots of it, and he thought the easiest way to get out of debt was to speculate. He bought shares in canal companies that never built canals and he bought western lands that proved worthless. He sold off some of his lands; he mortgaged his farms; he tried new business deals and new borrowings, but all in vain. Soon he was barricading himself from the people he owed, while the plantation at Stratford went to rack and ruin. He couldn't escape his creditors forever though, and one day, when Robert was only two years old, they came and put his father in debtor's jail. That was a curious practice of those days which did no good either for debtor or for creditor. If Anne Carter Lee hadn't had a little money of her own, things would have gone hard with the little family.

As it was they went badly enough. Light-Horse Harry managed to get out of jail in a year or so, but that didn't help much. It was clear that he would have to give up Stratford, now neglected and shabby, the garden overgrown with weeds, most of the Negroes gone. As a final gesture Anne Carter Lee with her little boy went out in the garden and planted a chestnut tree. Then the family set off for near-by Alexandria. Robert was just four years old, and he was never again to live in the great house or play beneath the towering trees.

Yet it wasn't a bad move — even from Robert's point of view. The little brick house on Cameron Street in Alexandria was pleasant enough, especially with some of the elegant furniture that had been brought from Stratford. The gardens were handsome and spacious, and Robert particularly liked the big snowball bushes. And there were two horses in the stables, so that of a Sunday Mrs. Lee and her children — there were two little girls now — were able to ride out in proper style.

Alexandria, too, was very much like home. It was filled with aunts and uncles and cousins, and no less than twenty of Light-Horse Harry's old soldiers lived there. All of these were proud to welcome their former commander and his family, and most of them were ready enough to tell young Robert stories of the exploits of "Lee's Legion." So Robert heard about men who were already legends — Marion the Swamp Fox, Sumter the Partisan Leader, the noble Marquis de Lafayette, and many others.

Mostly, though, the talk was about George Washington — or got around to him — for the spirit of Washington was everywhere in the old city. Wherever Robert went he saw houses and churches and taverns that brought up Washington's name. Here was the Masonic Lodge to which Washington had belonged, and the old Carlyle House where Braddock's expedition against the Indians had been organized. Here was Gadsby's Tavern,

9

where Washington had met so often with his fellow-revolution-
ists, still doing business. Here was the Friendship Fire Company, with a fire "engine" given by the General. Sundays
Robert went to Christ's Church and his mother would point out
Washington's pew.

Across the broad Potomac was the new city which bore
Washington's name, a straggling unfinished collection of houses,
strung out along muddy lanes where pigs and cattle jostled
the Congressmen. It was not nearly as handsome a town as
Alexandria. Also, not far down the river was Mount Vernon
where Washington had lived, and on pleasant spring days
Robert and his mother would drive down there and look at the

stately white-pillared mansion and the lovely lawns sloping down to the river. Up the Potomac just a few miles was the imposing new house called Arlington which George Washington Custis had built — Custis who was the adopted son of the first President of the Country.

Robert also heard stories of the Revolution from his father and his uncles and cousins, and sometimes his father read aloud from the History of the War that he was writing. That war was already a bit dim and awe-inspiring, like Washington himself.

Soon young Robert was to have a taste of war at first hand. In 1812 the United States and England fought a second time.

11

Robert's half-brother, Henry, marched off to Canada, as smart as you please in a major's uniform, and there was recruiting and mustering in of soldiers in Alexandria, as elsewhere. One hot summer day, when Robert was seven, he heard an explosion from the fort below Alexandria, and the next day there was the British fleet, its blue-coated sailors tumbling about the streets while their Commodore forced the city fathers to pay tribute as a price for sparing the town. That the Commodore meant business was clear enough, for the British had set Washington itself afire just three days earlier. Alexandria paid up, and was spared.

For a boy of seven all this was exciting enough, especially the fires in Washington that he could see from across the river. But soon the British left and were forgotten, and life went on its familiar way. It was, on the whole, a very pleasant way, pleasanter, certainly, than Stratford with its poverty. In the summertime Robert swam in the Potomac or visited his mother's kin at Shirley or Chatham; in the fall and winter he often went hunting, following the hounds afoot all through a frosty day. Perhaps it was more fun outdoors than in. For Robert's father was still dodging his creditors, still talking about his grievances, still scribbling away on his book. Meantime he was planning to get away to the West Indies or South America if he could. He found it hard to settle down to the humdrum existence of a sleepy little town.

One July day in 1812, just after the war with England had begun, Light-Horse Harry set off for near-by Baltimore to visit his friend, Alexander Hanson. Robert waved good-bye to him as he set off, a distinguished old man, elegantly dressed in a tall white hat and a long coat, with a white stock at his throat. The next Robert and his mother heard of him was that he was lying dead in a Baltimore jail. It wasn't quite true, but it was almost that bad. Somehow, no one knew quite how, he had got mixed up in a fight — he couldn't resist a fight. Gradually

12

the whole story came out, and it was one that made people hang their heads in shame. Alexander Hanson edited a newspaper which was against the war with England. The rabble of Baltimore thought this disloyal, and set out to punish him. It was while Lee was visiting him, that the mob swarmed down on Hanson's house, thirsting for blood. Lee thought that he knew how to handle a mob: a few shots would do the trick. But alas, a few shots simply maddened the mob. Just when things got serious, the militia arrived, and took Lee and Hanson and their friends to the city jail for protection. It proved a poor protection. The mob followed them, broke into the jail, attacked Lee and Hanson with clubs and knives, and left them for dead. Lee survived, but from then on he was broken in health and in spirit. More dead than alive, he made his way back home where his wife and children nursed him back to health.

Ironically enough President Madison now offered him a major-generalship in the armies fighting the old enemy. But Lee's fighting days were over. All he wanted was to get away to some warm climate where he could regain his health and find peace. President Madison was willing to help him, and

14

after a while passage was arranged — on an English boat, of all things. So one warm summer day in 1813 Anne Carter and her five children stood on the quay at Alexandria and waved a sorrowful farewell as Light-Horse Harry sailed by on his way to the Barbadoes.

Robert never saw his father again. For six years the old General wandered from island to island in a vain search for health. Every so often there would be letters with strange postmarks, and Robert's mother would read to her sons the stilted phrases which concealed so much anxiety and pride. "Self-command is the pivot upon which the character, fame, and independence of us mortals hang," or "fame in arms, or art, however conspicuous, is naught unless bottomed on virtue." Sometimes he would ask directly about the children. "Robert was always good," he wrote. "Does he strengthen his native tendency?"

That was an easy question to answer. Yes, Robert was always good, so good that if it hadn't been for his native manliness, he might have turned into a prig. More and more he took over management of the larder, the garden, the horses — Mrs.

15

Lee was becoming every day more of an invalid, and his sister Anne, too, was sickly, while Mildred was too little for anything but play. Carter, the oldest of the boys, was off at Harvard, and soon the next brother, Sidney Smith, went to sea as a midshipman. That left Robert pretty much in charge. In the quaint phrase of the time, he "carried the keys."

Meantime there was the serious business of an education — serious indeed for a boy whose family standards were so high, and whose prospects were so poor. For a time Robert had gone to one of the Carter schools; the family connection was so large that they kept up one school for the Carter girls and one for the boys. When he was thirteen his mother sent him to the Alexandria Academy — General Washington had been one of the trustees — where a genial Irishman named William Leary drilled him in Greek and Latin and mathematics. This would have prepared him for college, but there wasn't enough money for college. Brother Sidney Smith had made himself a career in the Navy; why shouldn't Robert have a career in the Army? Clearly, if he was to be a soldier, the place for him was the Military Academy at West Point. And to West Point he determined to go.

The first problem was to get into the Academy. The requirements for admission were easy enough, ludicrously easy by modern standards. Applicants had to be between the ages of fourteen and twenty, at least four feet nine inches tall, free from physical defects, able to read and write, and competent in arithmetic! Robert could meet these all right. He was seventeen years old, almost six feet tall, in perfect health, and as well educated as almost any boy of his age.

The real difficulty was to get an appointment from the Secretary of War who, at this time, was John C. Calhoun of South Carolina. Competition was sharp, especially in the South, where it was a tradition that the sons of gentlemen go into the Army. Yet Robert's chances were good. It was

16

not only that he was a handsome and likeable young man, well trained in the classics and in mathematics. That helped, of course. Rather it was that he had behind him the powerful Lee connection, and all their friends. And there were many who remembered Light-Horse Harry's services to his country, and who were eager to extend a helping hand to his son. So Robert was able to submit to the Secretary of War not only the usual recommendations from friends and teachers, but letters from no less than five Senators and three Congressmen! Whether it was these letters, or the Lee name, or young Robert himself, we do not know, but in March 1824 Robert E. Lee was informed that he had been appointed to the United States Military Academy at West Point.

On a warm June day in 1825 Lee stepped aboard a gleaming white paddle-wheeler — perhaps it was the *Chancellor Livingston* or the *James Kent*, or even the new *Richmond* — and steamed up the Hudson to West Point. It was only fifty-some miles from New York to the Point, but the trip took half a day, and there was plenty of time to admire the scenery, as lovely as any in the country. It was all new to Robert, yet not wholly strange, not unlike the upper Potomac, which he knew well — the broad blue river, on one side the steep Palisades, on the other trim lawns running down to the water's edge, and hand-

some mansion houses. The steamer stopped when it came opposite the Point, swinging back and forth in the current. A little skiff put out from the pier, and the lads who were going to the Academy climbed down the rope ladder and into the boat, and were rowed to shore, Robert among them.

Set in a great bend of the Hudson, the Point was as beautiful then as now. It was hemmed in on two sides by the majestic river; to the south stretched the Highlands, while Storm King Mountain, its summit often hidden in clouds, dominated the north. The magnificence of the natural setting brought out in sharp contrast the shabbiness of the Academy itself. As Lee came up the steep path from the river pier, he saw a group of ugly stucco buildings, squatting on a narrow, treeless plateau. There were the North and South Barracks, which housed the four-hundred-odd cadets, the main Academy building, a long mess hall — also used as a hotel for visitors — and, scattered around the grounds, a group of smaller buildings almost as ugly as the main ones.

Living conditions, Lee quickly learned, were as meager as the buildings. In the summertime Lee and his fellow cadets lived in tents, in what was called — in honor of the President then in the White House — Camp Adams. The rest of the year Lee lived in the old barracks. His room was small, bare, and uncomfortable, heated only by a tiny fireplace, and he had to share it with two or three other lads. Here he studied, in such time as was allowed him, by the flickering light of candles; here he slept, unrolling his mattress on a cold floor.   The food, too, as Lee soon learned, was very different from the rich and varied fare he was used to at home.   The Academy chef, a thrifty soul, filled his victims up on porridge, bread, soup, and potatoes, with bacon and mutton and beef only on rare occasions.   It was, all in all, pretty grim.

Plebe Lee fell quickly into the routine of the Academy. Reveille sounded at sunrise; then came drill and parade for an hour or so; breakfast; five hours of classes and study; an hour for dinner; two more hours of study; two hours for drill; supper, study, and inspection.   Taps were sounded at nine-thirty, and lights out at ten.   It was all quite strenuous, but once Lee got the hang of it, he managed easily enough.   There was not much time for play, and no organized sports at all.   Saturday afternoons and Sundays the cadets could swim in the Hudson, or walk to near-by Buttermilk Falls, or find a few hours for reading, and perhaps for visitors.

Life, as Lee soon learned, was hedged around with endless rules and regulations.   Woe betide the cadet who forgot them — who was late for classes or forgot to polish his boots or his buttons, who talked out of turn or failed in proper respect to instructors or to upper-classmen, or ventured off grounds in search for food or for forbidden entertainment.   Colonel Thayer, the Superintendent who had really made the Academy, was a strict disciplinarian, and failure to observe the rules was punished with demerits.   Too many of these, and out you went!

The academic requirements, too, were stiff.   Colonel Thayer had already established the rule, still an Academy tradition, that every cadet recite in every subject every day.   There was no such thing as falling behind in your work, and then boning up for examinations: if you fell behind, you fell out. The course of study was a narrow one.   The first year was

20

devoted to mathematics and French. Gradually other subjects were added — drawing, surveying, engineering, a bit of physics and chemistry, a smattering of history, geography, and "moral philosophy." There was also something called "the science of war" — a subject which Lee certainly mastered, whether at the Academy or elsewhere.

This was all theoretical, and you couldn't make a soldier by theory alone. Colonel Thayer knew that well enough: he was an engineer himself. So on top of all the book-study, there was constant drill, and practical training. The cadets learned how to handle artillery, how to build forts, how to lay out roads and build bridges, how to survey and make maps.

21

They were trained in tactics, and in the command of small groups of soldiers. All this was fun for the cadets: it took them out in the open, gave them a chance to ride horses, to use surveying instruments, to fire off guns, gave them a feeling that they were learning things of practical use.

Many a promising career was wrecked on the shoals of rules or grades. Of Lee's class of eighty-seven, almost half failed to graduate. But Lee had no difficulties either with the regulations or with his marks. From the beginning he was up among the first two or three in his class, and he held this position through the four years he was at the Academy. In his second year Lee was named staff sergeant, and asked to teach mathematics to the Plebes; thereafter he was both instructor and student. In his last year he won the most prized of all Academy distinctions — the position of Adjutant of the Corps. When he graduated he was number two in his class, and what is more, he had come through four years without a single demerit! As a "distinguished cadet" he could choose his own branch of service, and, like so many others, he chose the engineers.

To his classmates Lee was known as the "Marble Model." He may have been a model, but he was far from marble, far from cold and aloof, and there was nothing about him of the prig. Joseph E. Johnston — his classmate and later his ablest general — describes him at this time:

> We had the same intimate associates who thought as I did that no other youth or man so united the qualities that win warm friendship and command high respect. For he was full of sympathy and kindness, genial and fond of gay conversation, and even of fun, while his correctness of demeanor and attention to all duties, personal and official, and a dignity as much a part of himself as the elegance of his person, gave him a superiority that every one acknowledged in his heart.

Here we have the Lee of the future!

A full-fledged officer now, wonderfully handsome in his gray and white uniform, Lee returned to Virginia to visit with family and friends before taking up his professional duties. He came not a moment too soon. For Anne Carter Lee, long an invalid, lay at the point of death. Lee was with her when, a few weeks later, she died. All in all she had not had a very happy life. Her marriage had been a failure, she had been much alone, she had known poverty and sickness. But she had seen all her boys launched in life — Carter in the law, Smith in the Navy, and Robert, now, a lieutenant in the Army. She was proud of them all, as well she might be, and especially proud of Robert, who had been closer to her than any of her other children.

Robert lingered on to settle his mother's estate — what there was of it — and to visit about among his innumerable cousins at Ravenswood and Chatham and Eastern View. And there was another place he visited that summer.

The great white-pillared house at Arlington drew him like a magnet. There George Washington Parke Custis lived, the adopted son of Washington. He was an amiable old man who devoted his life to the memory of Washington, scribbling away at Fourth of July orations, painting pictures of Revolutionary battles, tending the many mementoes of Mount Vernon that had come to him, entertaining folk from Washington City across the river. Robert knew the place well. He had visited there often as a boy, for Mrs. Custis was a distant connection of the Lees. But now it was not Mr. and Mrs. Custis that he came to see. He had fallen head over heels in love with their daughter, Mary Anne Custis, and it was clear, too, that Mary's feelings for Robert were more than cousinly. She was a tall, pale, fragile girl, careless and easy-going, like her father, a bit spoiled, perhaps, but warm-hearted and affectionate.

Father Custis was far from enthusiastic about this courtship. Lee was an eligible enough young man, and his family as good as any, but he was, after all, only a poor second lieutenant, and — as the West Point song was to put it — "in the Army there's sobriety, promotion's very slow." Could Robert Lee support his daughter in the style to which she was accustomed on twenty-five dollars a month? Probably not. But, after all, Mr. Custis was a rich man and wanted only his daughter's happiness. And fortunately Mrs. Custis looked with favor on the match. So in the end Robert and Mary had their way.

There were delays, of course. Lieutenant Lee was ordered south to a dreary island off the Georgia coast, to work on the coastal defenses. It seemed dull work at the time, but came in useful later on when, as General Lee, he was in charge of the coastal defenses of the Confederacy. Next year he was ordered back to Old Point Comfort, in Virginia, to work on Fortress Monroe. It was pleasanter there — and besides he could get off for an occasional visit to Arlington.

Finally the wedding day was set, and Robert duly applied

26

for leave, and received a furlough. Brother Smith got himself a furlough from the Navy in order to be best man, and Carter came over from Washington, and all the Lee and Carter cousins descended on Arlington. When the great day arrived — it was the last day of June, 1831 — the rain came down in torrents. The poor clergyman, who had jogged through the country in an open carriage, was soaked to the skin, and had to be fitted out in what Mr. Custis could give him before he was able to perform the ceremony. But finally everything was straightened out, and Robert Lee and Mary Anne Custis were duly married.

It was to prove a very happy marriage. More than this, it was a marriage that meant much in history. For now Lee was heir not only to Arlington, but to everything that Arlington stood for. And what Arlington stood for was George Washington. Ever since boyhood Lee had heard about Washington, and in Alexandria he came to know Washington almost better than he knew his own father. And now he was to live with almost daily reminders of him — the portraits hanging from the walls, the china presented to him by the Society of the Cincinnati, the bookcase from his office, the very bed in which he died. More and more Lee came to model himself on Washington.

A soldier's life in peacetime is apt to be on the dull side. So Lee found it. Americans were interested in anything but war — anything but an Army and a Navy. Congress was stingy with the armed services. Lee had plenty to do, but not much to do it with. Sometimes he felt that he lived his life in a backwater, working patiently away at jobs that could never be properly finished, tinkering with coastal defenses here, keeping up fortifications there, falling into that routine which so often makes dullards. Gradually at first, then more swiftly, the years slipped by. He lost something of his debonair appearance, and became ever more dignified and impressive. He had, said a fellow officer who saw him at this time, a "noble and commanding presence." Fortunately much of his work was close to home — in the engineer's office at Washington, or at Fortress Monroe — and he was able to ride over to Arlington almost every day.

Lee's heart was in Arlington, the great house there, and the hundreds of acres of garden and farmland and woods, and, of course, best of all, his family. That family was growing fast. First there was a son, named George Washington Custis but called simply Custis. Then came Mary, then another son, William Fitzhugh, called "Rooney," then, in rapid succession, Anne and Agnes and Robert Edward, and finally Mildred — seven in all.

Sometimes Lee had to be away from Arlington — working at Fortress Monroe, or running the boundary-line between Ohio and Michigan, or sitting on a military court. Only once was he able to take his family along with him. That was when he went out to St. Louis, then in the Far West. That was quite a trip. First, the family stopped off at Baltimore where Lee had his portrait painted by a Mr. West — the earliest likeness we have of him. Then on they went, by the new railroad to Frederick, Maryland, by stagecoach to Pittsburgh, by boat to Cincinnati. There they stopped off to buy furniture for house-

28

keeping in St. Louis. It was lucky for them that they did. Their
boat went ahead without them — and blew up. That often
happened with the river steamboats of those days; it was one
of the chances that travelers took.

Lee's job in St. Louis put to a test all his skill as an engineer.
St. Louis was a thriving, bustling city, already the greatest in
the West, and its proud citizens looked forward to the day
when it would be the first city in the country. But its future
depended on the treacherous currents of the great Mississippi
River that flowed by its docks and wharves. That river had
brought it prosperity; now it threatened ruin. The swollen
Missouri, plunging into the Mississippi just a few miles north of
St. Louis, had cut a deep channel on the Illinois side of the river,
and piled up silt on the Missouri side. The silt had grown until
it became islands. If the islands kept growing, they would
block up the harbor of St. Louis — and that would be the end
of that city.

What was to be done? Lee set himself to saving St. Louis.
On paper the job was easy enough — just cut a channel on the
St. Louis side — but drawing plans was very different from work-
ing in the dangerous currents of the Father of Waters. First,
Lee built a long dike from the Illinois shore to the tip of the

30

northermost island. A newspaperman described this operation:

> The careful preparations were at last completed and everything in readiness: a number of flat-boats — some partially loaded with stones, others fully, according to the depth of the water in which they were to sink — moored with strong ropes from each, so that they could be cast loose to the current at one time by one stroke of an axe, and a plug in each so arranged that at a given signal all the plugs could be withdrawn simultaneously. A man stood ready at each line with a hatchet to cut loose; a watch in his hand, with the hour, minute and second indicated when to pull the plug. The signal to "cut loose" was the firing of the captain's pistol, which being given, as with one accord every rope was cut and the boats, exactly as calculated, swung out toward their proper and destined places. Curving at first by the greater force of the current, so accurately had every ounce of pressure been ascertained and provided for that when the moment arrived and every plug was withdrawn, the boats went down in a perfect line at right angles to the current as intended. Buoys were fixed, and next day Captain Lee paid an early visit to see if all was safe. All was safe, including the city of St. Louis.

The river struck this dike, and slid off around the islands. Now all the water of the Mississippi, forced into a narrow channel, washed away the sand in front of St. Louis.

Lee was three years on this job, but there were long stretches when the weather made it impossible for him to work, and he had a chance to see something of the West. He got to know St. Louis with its mixed population of French and Germans and Americans, Southerners and Yankees. The children, too, enjoyed life in this bustling western town. They could play along the banks of the river, or go on picnics into the near-by countryside. From time to time they saw brightly painted Indians who had come perhaps to call on old Governor Clark, who had gone with Lewis on that famous expedition to the Pacific, or just to see for themselves what the white man's world was like. Soldiers, stationed on frontier posts, clattered along the streets; tall raw-boned fur traders, who had spent years in the wilderness, sat around in hotels or bought supplies for a new trip. Emigrants, planning to push on to the rich farmlands of Missouri, stopped off to buy land or cattle. It was a new and exciting world.

As a reward, perhaps, for his work in St. Louis, Lee — a Captain now — was sent to Fort Hamilton in the harbor of New York. There he went, in 1841, with his family — and his cats, and a dog that he had saved from drowning and then adopted. He settled into a pleasant house that the government furnished him, and turned cheerfully enough to the many engineering tasks to be done in the harbor of the great city.

"American blood has been shed on American soil." So said President Polk in a message to Congress calling for a declaration of war against Mexico. History has not yet decided whether he was right or wrong. Abraham Lincoln, for one, thought that he was wrong. He was in Congress then, an obscure and ungainly representative from Illinois, just two years younger than Lee, and he introduced what came to be called the "spot" resolution, asking the President please to indicate the spot on American soil where American blood had been shed.

32

But all that was a question for the politicians, not for soldiers, and Captain Lee did not trouble himself about it one way or another. He felt that it was not a soldier's duty to decide the rights and wrongs of wars, but to serve his country whenever it called upon him. That decision was easy enough in 1846. In 1861 Lee was to take a different view. But then by 1861 Lee was an older and wiser man.

In that spring of 1846 Lee, like the true professional soldier that he was, welcomed the chance to see active service. He had been twenty-one years in the Army now, and never once seen an enemy or heard a hostile shot. Nor was he sure even now that he would have his chance. Week after week went by, while he read reports of battles at Palo Alto and Resaca de la Palma, in distant Mexico, of Kearney marching on Santa Fé and of Taylor hunting for Santa Anna, who was the Mexican general. But there were no orders for him. Sadly he said good-bye to fellow officers from Fort Hamilton and Governor's Island who went off to Mexico, while he went quietly about his duties. Would the war pass him by, leaving him an elderly officer doing a dull routine job, and forgotten by history?

Then, on August 19, came his orders. He was to report to General John Wool at San Antonio, Texas. Opportunity had come at last!

Or so, at least, it seemed. Lee had a pretty good idea of the military situation, and as he sailed for Texas he no doubt

33

planned what he would do to win fame and promotion. The
war had started on the Rio Grande, and it looked as if it would
be fought out in the desert wastes south of that river. There
General Zachary Taylor had gathered an army, and there he
had already met the Mexicans and defeated them in three hard-
fought battles — Palo Alto and Resaca de la Palma and Monterey. Indeed it looked as if the war might be over before ever
Lee got into it. But Santa Anna, the one-legged adventurer
who had fought his way to the Presidency of Mexico, was not
yet ready to quit. Somehow he had collected another army
and was preparing even then to renew the attack on General
Taylor.

Lee hoped to get to Mexico in time to see some of this fighting.
But there were many disappointments ahead. At a distance,
service with General Wool looked romantic enough. In actual
fact it proved a pretty dull business, dull and useless. Lee was
an engineer, and his job was to mark out roads, and build
bridges so that horses could drag the heavy guns across the
ravines and gulleys that cracked the earth everywhere. All this
he did well enough. It was more exciting to scout out the
enemy. But, alas, the enemy was elusive. Again and again
rumor swept the camp: the Mexicans are coming! Then Lee
would go out, sometimes alone, sometimes with a small force,
to try to locate the wily Santa Anna. But always in vain.
Sometimes Lee wished he were with General Taylor, so he could

see some real fighting. Wool's force was almost useless. Sometimes it seemed as if it were Wool who was lost, not Santa Anna.
Pretty soon it was a joke in the Army: "Where is General Wool?"

But in the end luck was with Captain Lee. President Polk
decided that the major attack on Mexico should be not across
the desert region south of the Rio Grande, but an invasion
from the sea and a stroke at the heart of the country, at Mexico
City itself. This great enterprise Polk entrusted to the commander-in-chief of the armies, General Winfield Scott — sixty
years old, fat, and fussy, but the greatest soldier the country
could boast. There would be plenty of work for the engineers
in any such invasion — marking out roads, preparing fortifications, locating batteries, doing reconnaissance, bridging the many
swift streams that coursed down the mountains. Captain Lee
was ordered to join this expedition, and with high hopes and
high heart he set off on his faithful horse Creole, across eighty
miles of sandy waste to the little post of Brazos on the Rio
Grande.

Brazos was all flurry and bustle and excitement. When he
got there Lee saw a vast camp of almost ten thousand men, and
off-shore more than a hundred ships bobbing up and down on
the waves — brigs, schooners, sailboats and steamers. Within
a month of his arrival the expedition got under way — the
biggest thing of its kind in American history, up to that time.
A little way down the Gulf it was joined by scores of new ships,

35

and on March 3 the whole flotilla sailed southward toward Vera Cruz, soldiers and sailors joining in singing,

We are bound for the shores of Mexico
And there Uncle Sam's soldiers, we will land, hi ho!

Or that popular favorite "Uncle Sam and Mexico," with its bold chorus:

Then march away, rum dum a dum
Then march away, rum dum a dum
Then march away, bold sons of freedom
You're the boys can skin and bleed 'em.

A few days, and the whole expedition was off Vera Cruz, gateway to Mexico. It was a stirring sight — the largest naval expedition in American history, the first sea-borne invasion in which Americans had ever engaged. There was music from the bands, singing and cheering, and much coming and going from ship to ship. When the Northers came howling in on the flotilla, many of the soldiers were seasick, and some of the sailors, too, but on the whole spirits were high. As they approached Vera Cruz, General Scott with his staff went ahead in a little vessel called the *Pedrita* to have a look. Bobbing up and down on the waves, the *Pedrita* was a perfect target for the Mexicans. Soon guns from the Fort began to boom. One shot landed just short of the boat, another went too far, a third burst directly overhead. It was a lucky thing for the Americans that the Mexicans were such poor shots. Had they hit the little vessel the whole expedition might have come to an end right there. And that would not have been the only change in history, either. For in the *Pedrita*, along with General Scott, were Robert E. Lee, Joseph Johnston, Pierre Beauregard, and George E. Meade. Had one of the Mexican cannonballs struck the boat the whole history of the Civil War might have been changed, for all of these officers were to be commanding generals in the armies that fought the Civil War.

Despite the hot reception of the *Pedrita*, all ten thousand of the American troops got ashore without a shot being fired at them. Three miles to the north of their landing-place lay the city of Vera Cruz, surrounded by high walls and ramparts, and defended by the frowning fortress of San Juan de Ulloa whose guns were trying their best to reach the American camp. What should Scott do — attack head on or lay siege to the town? A head-on attack on a fortified town would cost many lives. But delay, too, would cost lives and might fail. For the yellow-fever season was just ahead, and it was necessary, at all costs, to get the army away from the fever-infested shore and up into the hills. And there was always the chance that the wily Santa Anna might swoop down with an army to relieve the beleaguered city.

Lee, and most of the younger officers, favored a bold attack. But Scott overruled them, and decided on a siege. First, the Americans threw a great semicircle around the town, hemming it in from all sides. Then Captain Lee located the heavy guns. As army cannon were too light to reach the forts of Vera Cruz, Lee called upon Commodore Perry to help out with naval guns: Perry had fought in the war of 1812 and knew a thing or two about guns! These two-ton monsters were loaded onto smaller boats and ferried to shore, where soldiers hoisted them onto improvised wagons, and hauled them across three miles of sand and swamp to the locations Lee had selected. Meantime, the Mexican guns had found the range of the American camp and were pouring shells into the American lines. The soldiers were ready enough to protect themselves behind entrenchments, but most of the sailors thought digging trenches beneath their dignity — until taught better by Mexican fire!

After the battle, the navy Captain who had protested most strongly against building entrenchments met Lee, and apologized. "I guess you were right," he said. "I suppose the dirt did save some of my boys from being killed. But I knew that we would have no use for dirt banks on shipboard, that what we want there is clear decks and an open sea. And the fact is, Captain, I don't like this land fighting anyway. It ain't clean."

Within three weeks of the landings all the guns were in place, and all was ready for the attack. Two days of pounding ripped great holes in the walls of the doomed city. "The fire was terrific," Lee wrote, "and the shells thrown from our battery were constant and regular discharges, so beautiful in their flight and so destructive in their fall. It was awful. My heart bled for the inhabitants. The soldiers I did not care so much for, but it was terrible to think of the women and the children."

The Mexicans decided that honor had been satisfied and that they could now surrender. They raised the white flag, and the next day the whole garrison marched out and stacked arms. Scott had won his first victory in Mexico at a cost of only twenty men, and Captain Lee had won his first laurels.

By now the dreaded yellow-fever season had set in, and there was no time to lose. Within a week of the surrender of Vera Cruz, Scott had his men on the march toward Mexico City. It was a tough road — as tough as any American army has ever taken. Lee and his engineers went ahead — up into rugged and craggy mountains ten thousand feet high, criss-crossed with ravines and defiles and swift mountain streams, through country swarming with hostile Mexicans who were ready to shoot the invaders from behind ambush or to roll rocks down on them whenever they had a chance.

Up into the mountains toiled the American Army, expecting every day to run into the enemy. But no enemy appeared. Where was Santa Anna all this time? Rumor had him coming from all directions, each time with a larger force. Finally rumor proved true. Somehow he had managed to collect another army, and now he was hurrying from the capital down the National Road to meet the Yankee invaders. Early in April he reached the ranch of Cerro Gordo, and there took his stand in what seemed an impregnable position. On the one side was a rocky gorge "unscalable," wrote Lee, "by man or beast." On the other side rose a series of high hills, and on these Santa Anna planted batteries that commanded all available roads. Or so, at least, he thought.

What should the Americans do? A direct attack up the National Road would be suicide. An attack across the ravine was impossible. The only chance was to attack from the rear. Once again General Scott turned to young Captain Lee. Would he spy out the land, see if there was any way the army could take the Mexicans from the rear?

Off Captain Lee went across the rugged ground overgrown

42

with cactus, and strewn with giant boulders, working his way to the rear of the enemy encampment. Worse even than the terrain were the bands of Mexicans wandering about behind the lines. At one point Lee was almost caught. He had stopped at a spring for a drink, when he heard Mexicans approaching. Quickly he threw himself behind a large log, fortunately screened by thick underbrush. All day he lay there as Mexican soldiers came to the spring for water. One of them stepped over the log and almost on Lee, lying there breathless, suffering agonies from heat, insects, and thirst. Luck was with him, however, and when night came, he escaped. Next day he was out again, none the worse for his narrow escape. He cut a road to the Mexican rear, located his batteries, and prepared for an attack which should catch the enemy by surprise.

On the 17th and 18th of April, 1847, the attacks came off. Lee was in the thick of them. One column stormed the hill of Atalaya. "How far shall we charge them?" asked an officer. "Charge them to hell," answered General Twiggs. Another column hurled itself against the stronghold of Cerro Gordo itself, while a third swung around behind to cut off the Mexican retreat. By nightfall the battle was over and the enemy in full flight. Santa Anna himself left in such a hurry that he forgot not only his money but his wooden leg!

"You have no idea what a horrible sight a field of battle is," Lee wrote to his son. No doubt it was even more horrible to the defeated Mexicans whose losses ran into the thousands. Lee had covered himself with glory. He had been praised in all the despatches, even that of the Commander-in-Chief. "This officer greatly distinguished at the siege of Vera Cruz," wrote Scott, "was again indefatigable, in reconnaissance as daring as laborious, and of the utmost value." And, what was even better, Captain Lee was brevetted Major for his gallant conduct.

The very day after Cerro Gordo, Scott took the large city of Jalapa, and there he settled down to reorganize his army, bring up fresh supplies and re-enforcements, and give his soldiers a bit of a rest. They needed it. Scott and his staff made their headquarters at the Governor's Palace. There were garden parties and dancing on the lawns to the music of regimental bands; excursions to near-by ruins; plays by a hastily organized amateur theatrical company; and a bang-up Fourth of July celebration. All this was for the officers; the privates did not fare so well. There were no tents; no new issue of clothing; food was scarce; rains came down in torrents. The men got sick from strange food, bad whiskey, and perhaps from boredom. They called the place "Camp Misery."

Meantime there was work to do. Scott was headed for Mexico City — headed for the kill. If the capital fell, the war would be over. The hardest fighting was still ahead. Scott had to rebuild his army and bring up great quantities of supplies. Then there was the long march up across the mountains and down into the Valley where the capital lay — a march that promised the hardest kind of fighting.

Early in August the Army was in motion — ten thousand or

more men, with long supply trains, pack horses and mules, artillery and munitions, camp-followers and hangers-on strung out for miles along the National Road. More than three hundred years earlier "stout" Cortez had taken this same route, like Scott cutting himself off from his base, like Scott striking for the Halls of the Montezumas. A few days' stiff marching brought the Americans over the mountains and to a point where they could look down upon the mighty capital city, surrounded by lakes, circled by lofty mountain ranges.

"Not a man in the column," wrote General Scott, "failed to say to his neighbor or himself, 'that splendid city soon shall be ours.'"

But not without the hardest fighting that American armies had ever known. For the capital was heavily fortified by

46

nature and by man. It was all but surrounded by lakes and marshes, lava fields and rough terrain that made it difficult of approach, and it was protected by great stone walls and strong forts bristling with cannon. And inside the walls and the forts was a Mexican army larger than Scott's.

Now Scott faced the same problem that he had faced at Cerro Gordo. A head-on attack would cost him dearly — and might fail. Was there any way the Americans could circle around the outlying forts and attack the city from the rear?

Scott had learned by now to rely on Major Lee, and once more he called on him to scout out the ground. Skirting around the shallow lakes with the unpronounceable names, south of the capital, Lee came to a network of roads that straggled northward around the edge of a great lava bed, and led to the

47

outskirts of the city. Here, he reported, was the best approach. Scott accepted the advice, and set his army in motion toward the place Lee had picked out. The Mexicans quickly caught on to the new play, and they sallied forth to defend their capital. The fight for Mexico was joined!

Lee's most spectacular service came early in the campaign. Before the Americans could attack, they had to clear away the outposts that the enemy had hurriedly set up. The first of these was at the little village of San Geronimo on the other side of the dreaded lava field — the Pedregal as it was called. Across five miles of shaggy rock that looked like frozen ocean waves, Lee led the way to the rear of the Mexican army. He hoped to surprise the enemy. But this time it was the Americans who were caught by surprise. A Mexican force was bearing down on *their* rear. They were caught between two fires. What was to be done?

General Persifor Smith — he had won his laurels with old Zach Taylor at the battle of Monterey — decided that the only hope lay in an immediate attack on San Geronimo from front and rear before the Mexicans could bring up all their forces. But for that he needed more troops. He had to get word to Scott, get approval of his new plan, and get re-enforcements. Lee volunteered to recross the Pedregal, find Scott, and bring up new troops.

Night had fallen, and rain was coming down in torrents. Lee set off across the five miles of frozen lava, littered with giant boulders, overgrown with cactus and chaparral, gashed by deep ravines. Late that night he staggered into Scott's headquarters, soaked to the skin and ready to drop with fatigue.

"I am glad to see you," said Scott. "I've been trying to get in touch with General Smith — sent out seven messengers to him. Did any of them get through?" Not one had got through — only Lee.

In a few words Lee told the General about the situation at

48

San Geronimo and about the plan for the attack. Scott agreed to the plan and promised to send help at once. Back Lee went, across the terrible lava beds for the third time, to carry word to Smith waiting in front of San Geronimo. Thanks to Lee, the attack came off as planned. With fresh troops the Americans assailed the enemy front and rear. In less than twenty minutes it was all over, the Mexicans fleeing down the road to Mexico City. A fourth time Lee hurried back to Scott's tent with news of the fight and the enemy retreat. Scott saw how weary Lee was, but he needed him, and he sent him out to reconnoiter the road which the army should take in pursuit.

By noon of the next day the Americans reached the little

Churubusco River — really nothing but a drainage canal, but a sharp barrier to the advance nevertheless. It was tough work to get across it with enemy guns barking from the other side. Lee, who had been in action — riding and fighting — for thirty-six hours, led one of the attacking parties across the canal and to the outskirts of the capital.

The whole army shared in the glory of these battles of San Geronimo and Churubusco, but no one had distinguished himself more than Major Lee. General Scott called his dash across the Pedregal and back again "the greatest feat of physical and moral courage performed by any individual" in the whole campaign, and in his report on the battles he said that Lee was "distinguished for science and daring."

There was science and daring still to come. The outskirts of the capital had fallen, but the citadel itself had yet to be taken. The only approach was along a series of narrow roads across the lakes and swamps, all covered by Mexican guns. The other choice was a direct attack on the frowning fortress of

50

Chapultepec, the strongest fort in all Mexico. After consulting with Lee and other members of his staff, Scott decided to attack Chapultepec.

It was a tough nut to crack. Standing on a high hill, enclosed on three sides by heavy stone walls, and on the fourth by an outpost called Molino del Rey, it defied any army rash enough to assault it. First, Scott sent Lee to locate the batteries that were to prepare the way for the assault. Lee had already been up for more than thirty hours, and now he spent another sleepless night getting the guns in place and seeing that everything was ready for the great assault.

The attack was to start early on the morning of September 13. At dawn Lee took his place at the head of General Pillow's division, ready to guide it to the fort. With a great shout the American line moved forward, sweeping all before it as it stormed through a cypress grove, cleared a mine field under the very guns of the fort, and swarmed up to the walls of Chapultepec. Specially trained men hurried up with scaling ladders,

51

and swarmed up the ladders and onto the parapets, sending the Mexicans toppling from their stations or racing away in disorderly retreat. Meantime other columns of Americans had come up from the South and stormed into the fort. Assailed from two sides, the Mexicans struck their colors, and the victorious Americans pushed on into Mexico City itself.

Lee had not taken part in the assault. His business was to guide the army, and to carry messages back and forth from the Commander-in-Chief. As he dashed across the battlefield on one of his many errands, a bullet struck him. He kept going, not stopping even to have his wound dressed. For more than fifty hours he had fought and carried despatches. When the fort fell, he raced off to find the best way to lead the army to the city gates — and for the first and last time in his life, fainted.

The next morning he was up in time to see the capital surrender, and the Stars and Stripes hoisted over the Hall of the Montezumas. Santa Anna fled, Mexican resistance collapsed, and the war was over. There was glory enough for all. Lee found himself promoted to brevet Colonel and cited, once again, in all the despatches.

For some months he lingered on in the captured city doing routine work, making maps and surveys, hobnobbing with brother officers at the "Aztec Club," enjoying such social life as the capital afforded, and regaining his health and strength in the Mexican sunshine. Then, in May, he was ordered back

52

home. He sent a white pony ahead for his boys — what had happened to Creole we do not know. His own warhorse, Grace Darling, who had carried him through the thick of many battles, he took with him on the long trip to New Orleans and up the Mississippi and Ohio, then across the mountains to Washington and Arlington.

It had been almost two years since Lee had left home for the wars. When he had first sailed from Washington to join General Wool, he had been merely one of a large number of junior officers, neither more nor less important than the run of them. Less than a year of fighting had seen him promoted from Captain to Colonel, cited again and again in the dispatches, marked, above almost any other officer of the Engineer Corps, for a brilliant career. And in that year he had won the confidence of his brother officers and his superiors, above all of General Scott, in whose eyes he was a paragon of military virtues.

But the Mexican War brought Lee more than rank and glory. It gave him the training he was to need for the far greater trials that lay in the future. Now he had learned the real nature of war, and of command. He had come to know almost every one of the officers who were later to fight in the Union and Confederate armies. Three of them were to play a leading role in his own life: McClellan who was his first great opponent; Grant who in the end defeated him, and Joe Johnston whose command he took over at the crisis of the Civil War.

After the excitement of the Mexican War the next ten years seemed pretty tame. First Lee was given the job of building a new fort for Baltimore harbor. This was pleasant enough, what with so many friends and relatives in Baltimore. Lee welcomed the chance to settle down with his family and his friends, his dog Spec, and his Maltese cats. Spec was a special favorite. He had been the first to recognize Lee when he came home from the war, and the dog and the soldier were quite inseparable. Whenever his master was away, Spec pined; when his master was at home he went about with him everywhere, and he was fiercely jealous of the cats, on whom Lee lavished a good deal of affection.

On the whole Baltimore was pleasant if a bit dull. But there were moments of excitement. There was, for example, the time Lee was offered command of the Cuban revolutionary army. He thought hard about that, but turned it down in the end because he felt that he owed his services to the nation that had educated him. It is interesting to speculate on what might have happened had Lee accepted this glamorous offer. For the Cuban uprising ended in defeat, and its leaders died in front of a firing squad.

In 1852, while he was still struggling with the engineering problems of building Fort Carroll, Lee was told that he was to be the new superintendent of West Point Academy. This was a signal honor, and most soldiers would have rejoiced — but not Lee. He much preferred active service or, if he could not have that, service near enough to Arlington to take care of the Custis family and the family estates. But, as always, he took what duties were given him without a murmur, and in the summer of 1852 set out once more for the Academy which he had left, as a cadet, over twenty years earlier.

It was a very different Point from that to which he had first come a quarter century earlier. Most of the old familiar buildings were gone and most of the professors as well. The spirit was the same, however, and one generation of cadets was pretty much like another. Lee's eldest son, Custis — "dearest Mr. Boo," Lee called him in his letters — was here. His father had warned him against a military career, but he wouldn't be put off, and now he was leading his class, just as Lee himself had led his class. Custis's cousin Fitzhugh was at the Academy, too — you simply couldn't keep the Lees out of the army. Then there were many friends — Professor Robert Weir who painted Lee's portrait (Lee didn't like it very much) and a Major Garnett from Virginia and Major George Thomas, another Virginian who in 1861 went with the Union rather than with his state.

The three years at the Point were pleasant but uneventful. The duties of the Superintendent were exacting, but Lee found time for the social life he enjoyed, and for his family. Many an afternoon the cadets would see Lee cantering along on Grace Darling with his son Robert on a pony called Santa Anna. In the wintertime Lee would go out and watch Robert and the other Academy children sledding down the steep hills around the Academy grounds. There were always visitors to be entertained, and Sundays were given over to church and to teas for the cadets, most of whom were deathly shy. Lee was a strict disciplinarian, but he took a fatherly interest in all the cadets, watching over their health and welfare as well as over their studies. Nothing pleased him more than when a cadet did well; nothing grieved him more than the unhappy duty of sending home those who failed to keep up in their studies or to observe the rules of the Academy.

It was during these Academy years that two things happened that had a deep influence on Lee's whole life. In the spring of 1853 Mrs. Custis died. She had been a real mother to him,

and he loved her dearly. And that same summer, perhaps because Mrs. Custis's death had turned his mind more than ever to religion, he was confirmed in the Episcopal Church. Always deeply religious, the strain of piety in him now became stronger and stronger with every passing year. No one can understand the Lee of the Civil War years who does not realize how much he was the Christian Soldier, how sincerely he believed that Providence had ordered everything, and that men had to do only what was right, and leave the rest to God.

Lee made a good superintendent. He tightened up on the discipline, which had grown a bit lax. He introduced a few long-needed reforms and got some new buildings. He was respected and admired by the cadets and the faculty alike. Yet he felt all along that he wasn't cut out for this kind of life. He wanted active duty, life in the open, and he knew that the years were slipping by, and he was growing old and rusty in the service.

At the end of three years he was granted his wish for change. His old army friend, Jefferson Davis, was Secretary of War now, and eager to enlarge the army and give it more field training than it was getting. He persuaded Congress to provide for two new cavalry regiments, and appointed Albert Sidney Johnston Colonel and Robert E. Lee Lieutenant Colonel of one of them.

Lee accepted and was promptly assigned duty in Texas. So once more Colonel Lee was out where, not quite ten years earlier, he had been making reconnaissances for General Wool. It had been bad enough that time — all planning and drudgery, and no fighting. This time it was even worse. After all, he hadn't been long with General Wool, and there had been the exciting campaign with Scott. But this frontier duty that he was on now promised to go on forever, with never a moment of real excitement.

To be sure there were always the Comanches and the Mexican outlaws, who raided American settlements across the border. Every time Lee went after these, they vanished like a cloud. From time to time there would be a meeting with some miserable Indian chief who begged for presents — Catumseh, for example, who had no less than six wives to keep happy! But for the most part life on the frontier was just dull routine. Lee took long walks along the banks of the Brazos and the Rio Grande rivers; he studied birds; he kept a few hens and a kitten; he wrote long letters to his wife and children. Sometimes he would write about cats — his own and those of his fellow-officers:

> Can you not pack up and come to the Comanche country? [he wrote his little daughter] I would get you such a fine cat you would never look at Tom again. Did I tell you Jim Nooks, Mrs. Waite's cat, was dead? He died of apoplexy. I foretold his end. Coffee and cream for breakfast, pound cake for lunch, turtle and oysters for dinner, buttered toast for tea, and Mexican rats, taken raw, for supper. He grew enormously and ended in a spasm. His beauty could not save him. I saw in San Antonio a cat dressed up for company: He had two holes bored in each ear, and in each were two bows of pink and blue ribbon. His round face, set in pink and blue, looked like a big owl in a full blooming ivy bush. He was snow white, and wore the golden fetters of his inamorata around his neck in the form of a collar. His tail and feet were tipped with black, and his eyes of green were truly catlike.

60

It was when Lee was in San Antonio that he heard that his father-in-law, Mr. Custis, had died. He applied for leave to go back and comfort his wife and take care of Mr. Custis's estate, and as soon as leave was granted, he hurried home.

Now he was master of Arlington — and of other plantations as well — with almost two hundred slaves, thousands of acres, many plantation houses. All this, however, meant trouble rather than leisure or wealth. For Mr. Custis had been generous and easy-going. He had left large estates and large debts. As for the estates, they were badly run down. Lee saw that if he were to save anything, he would have to turn in and take care of things himself. He applied for a few months' leave, and the few months stretched into almost two years before he felt that it was safe to return once more to soldiering.

It was while he was on leave at Arlington, busying himself with the duties of a farm-manager, that he was suddenly ordered

to hurry to Harper's Ferry, at the fork of the Potomac and the Shenandoah rivers. A fanatical hater of slavery, John Brown, had raided the United States arsenal at Harper's Ferry, and the government feared a slave uprising. "Osawatomie Brown," the great gaunt leader of the anti-slavery forces who looked like a prophet out of the Old Testament, had been carrying on a one-man war in Kansas against the slave owners, and was planning a general uprising of the slaves. The plan fizzled out at Harper's Ferry, and Brown with a handful of men — his own sons and a few desperate Negroes — was cooped up in the arsenal there. With a detachment of marines under the leadership of a young lieutenant named "Jeb" Stuart, who was to be heard from later, Lee hurried out to Harper's Ferry. He found the situation well in hand. He demanded that Brown surrender unconditionally. When the old fanatic refused to surrender, Lee gave Stuart the order to rush the roundhouse, and in two minutes it was all over, with Brown and his men prisoners. It was a very small affair in Lee's career, but it showed him the danger that lay in the struggle between North and South over slavery.

That danger was a very real one. Every day the North and the South were pulling further and further apart. Every day misunderstanding and bitterness between the two sections grew. Every day the danger of secession and war came closer.

What was it all about? Like most professional soldiers Lee had never paid much attention to politics — that was a matter for the civilians. But he had heard all the arguments in his own household, at the Academy, or in the Army, where northern and southern officers were about equal in numbers, and where — during the years of peace — there was plenty of time for talk.

What was it all about? It was about slavery, of course. More and more Yankees were saying that slavery was a wicked thing, and that people who kept slaves were bad. Nobody likes to hear that he is bad, and certainly southern slave holders didn't think of themselves as particularly bad. Lee himself was a slave holder, and no one could call him a bad man.

The worst of it was that this slavery argument was all mixed up with the argument over "States' rights," and "the nature of the Union." Where were Southerners to look for protection of their "rights" — protection of slavery? Where but to the states. Slavery was a matter for each state to decide for itself, they said, and the national government had no business interfering with it, one way or the other.

Doubtless Lee had listened to hundreds of arguments over slavery and States' rights. He himself had little use for either. He had always disliked slavery. He set his own slaves free, and he was even now busy arranging to set free the two hundred or so slaves that he and his wife had inherited from Mr. Custis. He thought slavery was equally bad for the black man and the white man, and wanted none of it. Nor, for that matter, did

64

he put much stock in the fancy arguments for States' rights. The states had rights, of course. But what did that mean, after all? Did it mean that any state had a right to get out of the Union whenever it pleased? Lee didn't think much of secession, as it was called. Secession, he thought, was just a fancy name for revolution.

But that still didn't answer the question — what would he do if his own state of Virginia left the Union? That was a hard question — the hardest he ever had to answer. And it was hard for a very simple reason. It was a hard question because it forced him to choose between two loyalties — loyalty to Virginia and loyalty to the United States.

Lee was at once an American and a Virginian. His father and his kin had fought to make America a nation, and had been proud of what they had achieved. He himself had served since he was a boy in the Army of the United States. He had taken an oath of allegiance to the United States, and he had been proud to wear the uniform of an officer in the Army of the United States. In the war with Mexico he had risked his life again and again for the flag that he loved. And at the same time Lee was a Virginian. His roots were deep in the history of the Old Dominion. No family had contributed more to the making of Virginia than his own. No other numbered more members distinguished in her history. What should he do if Virginia seceded? Where did his duty lie? What was right?

65

After the John Brown affair Lee had been ordered back to Texas as commander of the Department of Texas, which meant that he was really in command of the whole Southwest. It wasn't much of a job, however, and there wasn't much to do but think. The Indians were giving trouble, here and there, and every so often a straggling band of Mexican bandits would come over the border and have to be chased back. But there was plenty of time, in the long days riding across the Texas plains or the long nights under the bright southern stars, to ponder the future of his country. Plenty of time to figure out where his own duty lay.

Plenty of time, it seemed, and yet not so much time as was needed. For the swift rush of events caught up with Lee, away there on the Mexican border. Not long after he had returned to Texas, South Carolina seceded. That was in December of 1860. Soon other states were following her lead. Even Texas was seething with the secession fever, Texas that had been so proud of coming into the Union on her own, so to speak.

People were asking him, "Where do you stand, Colonel Lee?" "What are you going to do?"

He knew where he stood, all right. He stood on the sidelines. He owed no loyalty to South Carolina or to Texas, or — for that matter — to the new Confederate States of America being organized at Montgomery in Alabama. He owed loyalty only to the United States and to Virginia, and as yet, thank Heaven, Virginia had not withdrawn from the Union.

66

"I wish to do what is right; I am unwilling to do what is wrong, either at the bidding of the South or of the North," he wrote to his son Custis, and urged him, at the same time, to think things out for himself and make up his own mind about where his duty lay. If only men would listen to reason, thought Lee; if only they would realize the dreadful dangers that lay ahead if they went through with this wicked business of breaking up the old Union. He sat down and wrote to his beloved cousin, Markie:

> God save us from our folly, selfishness, and short-sightedness. . . . What will be the result I cannot conjecture. I only see that a fearful calamity is upon us, and fear that the country will have to pass through for its sins a fiery ordeal. I am unable to realize that our people will destroy a government inaugurated by the blood and wisdom of our patriot fathers, that has given us peace and prosperity at home, power and security abroad.

And then he added a sentence which made clear the course he himself would follow.

> I wish to live under no other government, and there is no sacrifice I am not ready to make for the preservation of the Union save that of honour. If a disruption takes place, I shall go back to my native state, and save in her defense there will be one soldier less in the world than now.

That was the stand he took, and from that position nothing could move him. There could be no greater calamity than the break-up of the Union, but "a Union that can only be main-

tained by swords and bayonets, and in which strife and civil war are to take the place of brotherly love and kindness, has no charm for me." If, in the end, Virginia withdrew from the Union, he would go with his state. He could do nothing else.

This was what he told his family and his friends. Soon he was where he would have to tell it to his commander, General Scott. For Scott had called him back to Washington, and it was clear that something was afoot. With heavy heart Lee made the long journey back — the journey which was to end, four years later, at Appomattox Court House.

Lee reached Alexandria on the first day of March, 1861. What should have been a joyful homecoming was saddened by the sense of coming tragedy. Everybody was talking about secession and about war; everybody was asking Lee what he was going to do. The very next day he rode over the bridge to Washington for a long talk with General Scott. Scott was even more worried than Lee, and he had cause to be. The old Union was breaking up. One by one the states of the South were withdrawing from the Union and joining the new Confederate States of America. The old army, too, was breaking up, southern officers resigning by the score to go with their states. Scott was particularly anxious that Lee shouldn't resign. He had long ago decided that Lee was "the greatest military genius in America" and he needed him badly in case war really came. Scott was commander of all the armies, but by now he was an old man — seventy-five years old — and so fat he had to be lifted onto his horse. Now he told Lee that if he stayed with the

68

Army, he would be second in command. That meant that Lee would actually command the troops in the field.

Lee told Scott what he had already told his wife and children. He wanted no part in war. If Virginia seceded, he would have to go with his state and his people, but except in defense of his state he never wanted to bear arms again. Then, sorrowfully, he rode back across the Potomac to Alexandria, and out to Arlington.

A couple of weeks later came his commission as permanent Colonel in the U.S. Army — signed by the new President, Abraham Lincoln. And that same day the mail brought a letter offering him a generalship in the Confederate army, even then being organized. Happily Virginia had not yet seceded, so Lee was free to accept the colonelcy and ignore the generalship. He was still free to choose.

But not for long. The next month — it was April, the loveliest of months, with the apple blossoms coming out and the lilacs — the Virginia convention met to consider the fateful question of secession. And just as it began to debate the question, Lee received a mysterious letter from Francis Blair, friend and adviser to President Lincoln. Again Lee mounted Grace Darling and rode across the Potomac to talk with Francis Blair in the handsome yellow mansion across from the White House. It was a momentous conference. For Blair told Lee what Scott had hinted at. The President was prepared to offer him field command of the armies of the United States with the rank of major general. Would he take the command?

69

There must have been a moment of temptation. Lee was still loyal to the old flag and to the nation to which he had given his whole life. Virginia was still in the Union. And here was the highest command he had ever dreamed of — here a chance to vault from an obscure lieutenant colonel to a major general in a single month. But if he was tempted, it was just for a moment. He gave Blair the same quiet answer that he had given so often before: if Virginia seceded he should return home, and "save in defence will draw my sword on none."

That very day Virginia did secede. This, Lee said sadly, was "the beginning of sorrow." It was, indeed, but it was also the beginning of greatness.

It was the first of June, 1862. Richmond, capital of the Confederacy, was in a fever of excitement. All day long there had been a coming and going of troops, couriers dashing to the front and back again with despatches, long lines of ambulances toiling into the city, filled with wounded and dead, the streets and squares crowded with men and women looking anxiously among the wounded for sons and brothers — and through it

70

all the muffled sound of firing from the battlefield just a few miles away. The city was swept with rumors: the army had won a great victory; the army had suffered a heavy defeat; McClellan was marching on Richmond; McClellan was bogged down in the mud; General Johnston was dead; he was wounded, he had been supplanted; General Lee had been appointed to command the armies!

This last rumor, at least, was true. With McClellan at the very outskirts of Richmond General Johnston had sallied forth to save the city. His plans had gone astray, and his army had suffered heavy losses, but McClellan had been checked. In the fighting Johnston had been badly wounded and President Davis, who had himself gone to the front, had turned at once to Lee and given him supreme command.

That very day Lee issued his first Special Order — and baptized the army with the name it was to carry to deathless glory:

> The existence of all that is dear to us appeals in terms too strong to be unheard, and I feel assured that every man has resolved to maintain the ancient fame of the Army of Northern Virginia.

It was more than a year, now, since that fateful day in April, 1861, when the batteries of Charleston had opened fire on Fort Sumter, and the great war had begun. Fort Sumter had fallen easily enough, the Stars and Stripes fluttering down, while the men and women of Charleston shouted themselves hoarse with joy. After that things weren't quite so easy for the South. In the beginning all had gone well. From Virginia to Texas, every state had joined the new government, and patriotic Southerners had rallied by the tens of thousands to the new flag, the Stars and Bars, and marched gaily off to war. The North, too, had girded itself, but more slowly, and with less ardor. The first major test had come at Bull Run, just across the Potomac in Virginia, and the Confederates were victorious. For a moment it seemed as if the war might end, then and there. But defeat

aroused the fight in the Yankees, and after Bull Run they settled down to business in dead earnest. Gradually, through 1861 and into 1862, the immense superiority of the North in men and arms and money made itself felt. And gradually, too, Abraham Lincoln was getting command of the situation, winning the support of a North that had been divided, inspiring men to fight for the old Union.

The year 1862 had opened badly for the Confederacy. Farragut captured New Orleans; Grant carried the war into Tennessee and Alabama; western Virginia was in Federal hands. And now Lincoln had raised a mighty host and, under the leadership of George B. McClellan, Lee's comrade in Mexico, it had landed on the peninsula below Richmond and worked its way slowly up the James River. Now this great army, 115,000 strong, stood at the very gates of the capital. Dark days for the Confederacy!

Could Lee save Richmond? This was his first opportunity to show what he could do. When Virginia seceded he had gone with his state, just as he had said he would, and his state had given him command of all its military forces. Yet during the first year of the war he had been something of a disappointment.

When Virginia joined the Confederacy her troops became part of the Confederate army. President Davis, whose confidence in Lee was boundless, sent him first to the mountains of western Virginia, where geography, bad weather, and lack of supplies, all combined to make his campaign a failure. Then Davis sent him south to strengthen the defenses of the Carolinas and Georgia — work for which his training as an engineer and his experience thirty years earlier had specially fitted him. In March, 1862, when McClellan began his campaign on the peninsula, Davis recalled Lee and appointed him "general in charge of military operations under the direction of the President" — a position that might mean a great deal, or nothing at all.

74

Had it not been for the wounding of General Johnston it might have meant nothing at all. But when, late in the night of May 31, 1862, Davis and Lee rode back through the tangled woods and thickets around the village of Seven Pines and Davis told Lee that he was now in command, the whole history of the Civil War was changed.

Could Lee save Richmond? The capital was beleaguered on all sides. Picture to yourselves Richmond as the hub of a wheel, whose rim stretched in a vast semicircle from the mountains and valleys of western Virginia to the mouth of the James River on the east. From this rim a series of imaginary spokes led down to the hub at Richmond. At the head of each of these spokes stood a Federal army which might move down along them on to the capital. One army was in the Valley of Virginia; another stood poised at Fredericksburg just fifty miles to the north; a third, the most powerful of all, had worked its way up from the mouth of the James and was now a scant seven miles from the city.

To meet all these armies Lee had only 80,000 men. More were coming, to be sure. Companies from Louisiana and Texas and Georgia were swinging jauntily through the streets of Richmond on their way to the front, the boys — most of them still in their teens — cheering and waving their hats as they passed the bands playing "Dixie" or "Bonnie Blue Flag." Batteries of artillery were rumbling along the streets, drivers whipping their horses to a trot. Wagons loaded down with ammunition, with food, with medicines and bandages, lunged along the side streets, headed for the army in the field.

With his smaller forces how could Lee meet three hostile armies? He had already worked out a plan to stop the invaders — stop them, roll them back, and destroy them. It was a plan which involved a series of intricate moves, as on a chess board. It was in the execution of this plan that Lee's military genius first appeared. That genius was, above all, offensive. He was to prove himself a great soldier on the defense, but it was in carrying the fight to the other fellow that he was supremely great. Now confronted by three armies he refused to stand on the defense, but planned instead to strike — to bewilder, scatter, and destroy the enemy.

The first part of Lee's plan was to tie up the two armies in the North — the one in the Valley and the one at Fredericksburg — so that he could deal separately with McClellan. How could he do this? His plan was to strike north up the Valley, scatter the Federals there, and threaten Washington. With Washington in danger, he was sure that Lincoln would pull back the army at Fredericksburg to defend the capital — thus leaving him free to deal with McClellan alone.

76

Fortunately Lee had, in the Valley, a general who could be trusted to understand this plan and carry it through — Stonewall Jackson. And now Jackson comes on the scene — the mighty, the incomparable Stonewall, whose fame is forever linked with that of Lee. He had won his name at Bull Run when a General rallied his men: "There stands Jackson like a stone wall." A rock in defense, he was greater still in attack — the greatest master of the swift march, the surprise, the bold sortie, the quick withdrawal, in all our history. He was a man after Lee's own heart, bold, brave, firm, reliable, stern, a devout Christian, who would not march or fight on Sunday if he could help it, and an inspiring leader. Lee trusted him and he worshipped Lee.

"Lee is the only man I know whom I would follow blindfold," Stonewall said.

Lee's plan went like clock-work. First, Jackson took the offensive. In a wonderful campaign he swept up and down the Valley, meeting and defeating one by one three separate Federal armies, and scaring the daylights out of Lincoln and his advisers. Not only did the Federals pull back from the Valley but word went out to the Union general at Fredericksburg to come north

and protect the capital. It was all just as Lee had planned it. Now Lee had only McClellan to deal with. And Jackson hurried down from the Valley to help in the battle for Richmond.

General Lee wanted to know just where McClellan had his great army, and what he was up to. He turned to his young friend Jeb Stuart—Beauty Stuart he was called because he was so ugly — and asked him to take his cavalry and get the information. With light heart Stuart and his men rode clean around McClellan's army and brought back the information Lee needed, sending a thrill of joy all through the Confederacy.

Now Lee's plans were complete. McClellan, who had not expected to be attacked, had spread his army from the James River to across the muddy Chickahominy which flowed into it below Richmond. With the Union army thus divided, Lee struck a whole series of hammer blows that go by the name of the Seven Days campaign. The first blow was at the Federal right, the second at the left. Lee sent one branch of McClellan's army rolling up the Chickahominy; he sent another stumbling back from that river to the protection of near-by swamps and woods. Mechanicsville, Gaines's Mill, White Oak Swamp,

Savage Station, Frayser's Farm, Malvern Hill — every day a fierce new blow, every day a new name for the regimental battle flags. McClellan's scattered army reeled back and back until it reached its camp on the James River. There the Federals dug sullenly in, while Lee gave his own exhausted army a brief rest.

It had been just a month since Lee took command. What a change in the scene! Then the Federals were hammering at Richmond, the capital seemed doomed, and the Confederacy itself was tottering. Now Richmond had been saved, the Valley had been cleared, the Federal army had given up the attack and was in retreat. With inferior forces Lee had beaten the largest army ever assembled in the western hemisphere.

Lee had no intention of resting on his laurels. McClellan

still stood on the James River, licking his wounds, but almost a hundred thousand strong. And north of Richmond another vast army was assembling. Lincoln called General John Pope to command this army. "I have come from the West," said the boastful Pope, "where we have always seen the backs of our enemies; from an army whose business has been to seek out the adversary and to beat him when he was found." Would he seek out Lee — and beat him?

That is doubtless what he intended to do, but Lee didn't propose to give him a chance. Even as Pope was slowly getting ready to move on Richmond, Lee planned to seize the offensive. He had to keep one eye on McClellan, to be sure, but he thought that once he started after Pope, Lincoln would hastily recall McClellan to the defense of Washington. That is just what happened. With a great pretense of secrecy, Lee divided his army in two. First he sent Jackson back to the Valley with part of it; with the rest he started north after Pope. Pope rose to the bait. He called loudly for re-enforcements from McClellan, then went after the elusive Jackson.

That was just the way Lee had planned it. It was a bold move to divide his own army in the face of a superior enemy. But Lee had one immense advantage. Geography was on his side. He had the inside — the shorter — lines, and could move his troops back and forth with ease, while the Federals had to move around the rim of the wheel. And Jackson knew the Valley as he knew his own backyard. He could race up and down it, slipping in and out of its narrow passes as he pleased, surprising and confusing the Federal generals.

Pope thought he was the hunter. Actually he was the hunted. Lee timed his operation perfectly. When all was ready, Jackson emerged from one of the gaps in the mountain onto the battle-field of the first Bull Run and began a skirmish with one of Pope's divisions. Thinking he had Jackson trapped, Pope turned his whole army against him. Then, while Pope was snarled up with Jackson, Lee fell on him from the rear, struck him and all but destroyed him. The result of this second battle of Bull Run was not just a Federal defeat, it was a disaster. Within a few days Pope's army was in full retreat. Some of the regiments didn't stop running until they reached Washington.

It was just ten weeks since Lee had taken command. In that time he had defeated one vast army under McClellan and forced it to withdraw. He had defeated another army under Pope, and sent it sprawling back north. Stonewall Jackson had cleared the Valley. All Virginia was freed of the enemy, and Washington, not Richmond, was in danger.

Now, with the Federals on the run, was the time to clinch the victory. Lee had outwitted McClellan twice by pretending to threaten Washington. Now he could really threaten Washing-

ton. He was always for taking the offensive, and here was his chance to give the Yankees a taste of what Southerners had so long endured. "We cannot afford to be idle," he said to President Davis, "and though weaker than our opponents in men and military equipments, we must endeavor to harass if we cannot destroy them."

He was determined to destroy them if he could. Within a few days of the victory at Bull Run, Lee's veterans were swinging up the hot dusty roads of northern Virginia, splashing across the

fords of the Potomac, and scrambling up onto the soil of Maryland. Regimental flags were whipping in the breeze, regimental bands were playing an old familiar tune to which the soldiers sang new words:

> Thou wilt not cower in the dust
> Maryland, My Maryland!
> Thy beaming sword shall never rust,
> Maryland, My Maryland!
> Remember Carroll's sacred trust,
> Remember Howard's warlike thrust
> And all thy slumberers with the just,
> Maryland, My Maryland!

It was a ragged, unkempt army, most of the men lean, dirty, and cadaverous, their uniforms in rags, some with toes sticking out of their shoes, others limping along barefoot. But there was

a dash about them, all the same. It was a victorious army, sure of its cause, confident of its destiny, devoted to its leaders — and above all to "Marse Robert."

The long columns swung along the Maryland roads. One was headed for Pennsylvania, the other, under Stonewall Jackson, veered off to capture Harper's Ferry. Then fortune played a scurvy trick on Lee. A Confederate officer dropped a copy of an order, telling the whole plan of the campaign. It was picked up and taken to McClellan. Now the Union commander knew just what Lee's plans were and, what was more, he knew that Lee had divided his little army. For once McClellan moved swiftly, to catch Lee while Jackson was still at Harper's Ferry. By good luck Lee got wind of what had happened, and sent a hurry-up call to Jackson. Leaving a division at Harper's Ferry under A. P. Hill, Jackson hurried back to rejoin the main force just in the nick of time. For where Antietam Creek joined the

Potomac, McClellan with 80,000 men had caught up to Lee who, even with Jackson, had only 40,000. Outnumbered two to one, what should Lee do? He could retreat, or he could fight it out.

He chose to fight. And so there on the rich Maryland countryside, with its white frame houses and great red barns, its fields of wheat and of corn, and its little patches of woods, was fought out the battle which would determine the fate of the Union.

Lee took up his position on the gentle slopes between the Antietam and the Potomac. McClellan massed his giant army on the other side of the little stream. If he could defeat Lee now, or get between him and the Potomac, he might bag the whole Confederate army.

All day long the boys in blue hurled themselves at the thin gray lines stretched out in a great semicircle in the meadows and woods overlooking the Antietam. All day long the boom of two hundred cannon reverberated up and down the lovely valley. "The carnage," said Stonewall Jackson, "was terrific." Again and again it seemed as if the Federals would break through; again and again the Confederates threw them back. Stonewall was living up to his name at one end of the line; Longstreet clung to the other; D. H. Hill hung grimly on to the center. Lee sat astride his beloved gray horse, Traveller, calm and collected, watching every move, encouraging the fighters, consoling the wounded. At the height of the battle one battery, reduced to a single gun, its gunners exhausted and dazed, with-

86

drew from the firing line. Lee told their captain to go back
to the front. "General," said one of the grimy gunners, "are
you going to send us in again?" "Yes, my son, you must all do
what you can to help drive these people back." The gunner
was Robert Lee, junior, and like a good soldier he went back
into the fight.

By mid-afternoon the superior power of the Federals was
beginning to tell. The left and center of the Confederates,
battered and mangled as they were, hung grimly on, but the
right was in desperate danger. There the Yankees had finally
forced the Antietam and were moving irresistibly up the slope,
swarming into the exhausted Confederate lines. If they suc-
ceeded, they would put themselves between Lee's army and the
Potomac, and then it would be all up with Lee.

Could the Confederates hold out until darkness fell? Not
without re-enforcements. And re-enforcements were on the way.
Early that morning, A. P. Hill had started from Harper's Ferry
and all day long he had kept his division on the run. At four
o'clock Lee saw a cloud of dust off to the right, and soon the
red flags of the Confederacy were streaming towards the battle-
field. Hill had come at last! On the double-quick now, his
men broke through the wheat fields and raising their voices in
the long rebel yell, they hurled themselves on the advancing
Yankees. The Federal line stopped, crumpled up, and rolled
back down the hill. The day was saved. It had been the
bloodiest day of the war.

Outnumbered two to one, Lee had fought McClellan to a standstill. The next day the two armies stood, facing each other defiantly, neither willing to renew the fight. Then, under cover of night, Lee withdrew to Virginia. The first invasion was over.

With Lee back in Virginia, and the North safe, the cry went up once more, "On to Richmond." McDowell, McClellan, Pope — all had tried and all had failed. This time Lincoln turned to General Burnside — now remembered only because of the peculiar type of whiskers he wore, later to be called burnsides, or sideburns. That winter Burnside led a mighty Union army of 125,000 down the familiar road towards Richmond. Lee took his stand at Fredericksburg, on a height overlooking the broad Rappahannock, and waited for him.

The battle came on a bitter day in mid-December of 1862. As the fog lifted, in the early morning, a pale sun showed the Union army massed at the edge of the river, and the Confederates entrenched on Marye's Hill and Strafford Heights behind the town of Fredericksburg. At a signal the Federal artillery thundered out, and long lines of blue started up the slopes toward the Confederate entrenchments. They were thrown back. On they came, again, and once more deadly fire from the Confederate trenches tore great holes in their ranks. Four more times during that dreadful day the Union regiments marched up the heights to certain death, until at last even the Confederates broke forth in cheers at their bravery. Astride Traveller, Lee watched the Union rout. "It is well that war is so terrible," he said, "we should grow too fond of it."

Could no Union commander defeat Lee? Almost in despair Lincoln turned to General Hooker who had won the nickname "Fighting Joe" for his gallantry in the Peninsula campaign. "My plans are perfect," said Hooker to his officers. "May God have mercy on General Lee, for I will have none." His "plans" were, it seemed, the same as those of Pope and Burnside

90

— a head-on advance against the Confederates. Well might he feel confident, for his army had been increased, now, to almost 140,000 while Lee had less than half that number.

And so, at the end of April, 1863, the Union army once again headed south — across the Rappahannock and its little tributary, the Rapidan, towards Richmond. It was springtime in Virginia — and that meant mudtime, and the country into which the Federals advanced was a tangled region, criss-crossed by streams, dotted with swamps and marshes, overgrown with bushes and second-growth timber — country which richly de-

91

served its name, the Wilderness. Here Lee was on home ground. He was sure that once Hooker was tangled up in the Wilderness, he would be an easy mark.

So once again Lee did what he had done so successfully against Pope. In the face of a superior enemy, he divided his forces in two. Jackson was sent off, with 28,000 men, on a broad sweep around Hooker's right, while Lee himself stood with only 14,000 to lure Hooker further on into the Wilderness. On the night of May 2nd Jackson plunged into the right side of Hooker's army and threw it into disorder. At the same time Lee attacked the enemy front. Confused and dazed the Union army fell back, and the next day the General who was going to have no mercy on Lee, gave the order to retreat. It was, in some ways, Lee's greatest victory.

But it was a victory purchased at a high price. On that dark night of the 2nd, in the tangled undergrowth of the Wilderness, where it was hard to tell friend from foe, Stonewall Jackson was shot by one of his own men. "He has lost his left arm," wrote Lee, "but I have lost my right." He had, indeed. Within a week the matchless Stonewall was dead. From that day forward the sun which had shone so brightly on the Confederate cause began to set.

Lee realized this, better than most. Tennessee had been over-run; the great fortress of Vicksburg, last link of the Confederacy with the West, was under siege. Every day Yankee ships were drawing the sea blockade tighter and tighter. But if Lee took a gloomy view of the prospects of the South, he gave no outward sign of it. He had thrown back four giant armies, and now once again he was ready to take the offensive. While Hooker pulled back across the Rappahannock, Lee recalled his "warhorse" Longstreet from the South, and prepared, once more, to carry the war to the North.

It was June of 1863. A haze of heat shimmered over the fields of northern Virginia, and the dust rose in clouds as Lee's legions, 75,000 strong, wheeled into the Valley and headed north. Unopposed, they crossed the shallow Potomac, swept through the narrow strip of Maryland, and struck at the heart of Pennsylvania. What would Lee do? He could drive straight on for Harrisburg, the capital of the state, or he could turn east and attack Washington itself.

Then he made a serious mistake — the most serious, as it proved, of his whole career. Twice Beauty Stuart had ridden clean around the Union army, and now he wanted to do it again. Lee let him go. And so, at this critical moment, Lee was deprived of his "eyes." Without his cavalry he didn't know where the Federals were or what they were doing. Of course, he hoped that Stuart would be back in time with just this information. But Stuart ran into bad luck and before he could fight his way back, the Union army had caught up with Lee. The crisis of the Confederacy was at hand.

That was the battle of Gettysburg. Had Lee known what was in the enemy's mind, had he been able to pick his own ground, he would never have fought at Gettysburg. He had planned to take up a strong defensive position on a slope near the little village of Cashtown. But on June 30 part of his advance guard, mostly barefooted as always, strayed into the old town of Gettysburg in search of boots and shoes, and there ran head-on against Union cavalry. There was a skirmish;

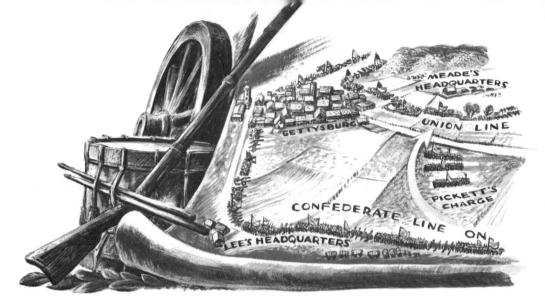

each side threw in re-enforcements, and the battle of Gettysburg was on.

The setting was much like that of Antietam a year earlier. It was mid-summer in southern Pennsylvania; a blazing sun beat down on fields and orchards, and not far away was the town with its red brick houses, its steepled churches, and its little college. Stretching southward, like two great parentheses, were Seminary Ridge and Cemetery Ridge, on whose grassy slopes the battle was to be fought — fought with such savage fury and such heroism as will be remembered as long as the history of the nation is remembered. Seminary Ridge and Cemetery Ridge, Big Round Top and Little Round Top, Culp's Hill, Devil's Den and the Peach Orchard — even now, after nearly a century, these names are other words for valor.

In their ragged gray and butternut uniforms (gray cloth had become hard to get), the Confederates massed along the slopes and in the woods of Seminary Ridge, the Stars and Bars and scores of regimental flags pointing proudly to the skies. Less than a mile to the east the Stars and Stripes showed where Meade's army had entrenched itself along Cemetery Ridge. Lee had either to attack or retreat. He had not invaded the North to retreat, so he attacked.

94

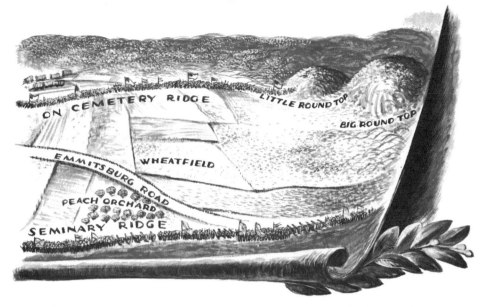

The first day went well for Lee, though Federal troops seized the two Round Tops. Lee planned to drive them off by attacking at dawn the next day, but Longstreet — to whom the attack had been entrusted — was late in starting. When he did attack, the Federals were firmly dug in on Little Round Top and could not be dislodged. The third day's fighting told the tale. Once again Lee planned to hurl Longstreet's corps against Cemetery Ridge in the early morning; once again there were agonizing delays and the Federals strengthened their lines. At one o'clock the Confederate artillery opened up on the enemy all along the front, and the Union cannon answered shot for shot. Then, when the fire slackened, General Pickett prepared to lead all that was left of the unengaged forces of the Confederate army in a desperate charge.

"Up, men, and to your posts," he called out. "Don't forget today that you are from old Virginia."

General Armistead, who was to lead the advance, rode up to his color guard. "Sergeant," he said, "are you going to put those colors on the enemy's works today?"

"I will try, sir," the color bearer replied, "and if mortal man can do it, it shall be done."

95

With a long rebel yell three lines of gray emerged from the wooded ridge and swept up the long grassy slope to where the Union gunners stood waiting. It was a stirring sight: eighteen thousand men, their bayonets gleaming in the sun, their banners fluttering in the breeze, advancing almost as on parade. There were some moments of silence. Then all along the ridge the massed Federal cannon opened up, tearing great gaps in the Confederate ranks. The line seemed to melt away, but the survivors closed up and came on, nearer and nearer, until they swarmed up to the top of Cemetery Ridge in one crowding, rushing line. With cap raised on the point of his sword General Armistead leaped the stone wall into the Union lines, and his color sergeant planted the barred flag of the Confederacy atop the ridge. A hundred men followed the flag into the Union lines. Then a great wave of blue swept over them and overwhelmed them, and Pickett's charge passed into legend.

Lee sat astride Traveller watching it all, watching that miscarriage of his plans which spelled disaster to the cause he loved. No word of complaint passed his lips, though after the war he said: "Had I had Stonewall Jackson at Gettysburg, I should have won that battle."

An English officer who was with Lee described him as he was at the close of the battle:

> He was engaged in rallying and in encouraging the broken troops and was riding about a little in front of the wood, quite alone. His face, which is always placid and cheerful, did not show signs of the slightest disappointment, care, or annoyance; and he was addressing to every soldier he met a few words of encouragement, such as "All this will come right in the end; we'll talk it over afterwards; but in the meantime all good men must rally. We want all good and true men just now." He spoke to all the wounded men that passed him, and the slightly wounded he exhorted to "bind up their hurts and take up a musket." Very few failed to answer his appeal, and I saw many badly wounded men take off their hats and cheer him.

And to one of his generals who came to report, Lee said, "Never mind, General, all this has been my fault — it is I who have lost this fight, and you must help me out of it the best way you can."

It was high tide for the Confederacy, and thereafter all was ebb tide. The next day Lee moved his army southward to the Potomac. The Federals, though victorious, had been so badly mauled that they did not dare follow, and Lee made good his retreat to Virginia. "May God guide us and protect us all, is my constant prayer," he wrote his invalid wife. And to President Davis he sent an offer to resign his command. "I alone am to blame," he said. Needless to say, Davis refused his resignation. It was not only that he loved and admired Lee; he knew that without Lee the Confederacy was lost.

For Lee and his Army of Northern Virginia there was little further fighting that year. It was not only that the army had been thinned out by the losses of the Gettysburg campaign. Besides that the Confederacy had lost heavily in other theaters of the war, and there was no chance for re-enforcements. The soldiers that were left in the Army of Northern Virginia — "Lee's Miserables," as they called themselves in grim jest — had hardly anything to fight with. Thousands were barefoot, and

all were without overcoats, blankets, or warm clothes for the biting winter. Food, too, was short. Sometimes companies would go for whole days on nothing but hardtack and a bit of salt pork. Lee shared their privations. Like his soldiers he lived in a tent in the open, went without heat or other comforts, made his dinners off a potato and a slice of salt pork.

The Federal armies suffered no such shortages, neither of men nor munitions nor equipment nor food. Yet their general, Meade, had had enough of Lee for the time being. He was not anxious to renew the fight after Gettysburg — not on Virginia soil, in any event.

For almost a year after Gettysburg, there was no heavy fighting in the East. While the armies of Lee and Meade licked their wounds, the main theater of the war shifted to the West. Grant took the great fortress of Vicksburg and Lincoln could say "the Father of Waters goes once more unvexed to the sea." A few months later Generals Grant, Sherman, and Thomas smashed the Confederates at Chattanooga, and the way was open for a sword thrust at the heart of the South. That next spring of 1864 Sherman began his advance on Atlanta. Lincoln called U. S. Grant east, and made him commander-in-chief of all the Union armies.

Could the stricken Confederacy hold out? Every day the Union was growing stronger, every day the Confederacy was growing weaker. No longer could Lee hope to take the offensive — Lee, who was the greatest offensive fighter America had ever known. Now his only hope was to stand on the defensive, beat off every Federal attack, wear the Union armies down. Somehow he had to persuade the North that it could never subdue the South and that it might as well quit trying.

By the spring of 1864 the winter floods had gone down, and the muddy roads of Virginia were drying out. Grant had built the Union army up to 130,000 men, and collected all the arms and food that he needed for a long campaign. Now he prepared to try once more, where so many had failed. Did the ghosts of McClellan and Pope, Burnside and Hooker haunt him as he launched that army against the indomitable Lee? Probably not: in any event Grant was not a man to be frightened by ghosts. A sharper contrast than that between Grant and Lee could scarcely be imagined. Lee was an aristocrat, stern and just but tender and humane, beloved by his men as no other general on either side. Grant was rough, careless of his dress, modest, and no man to give up, or even to worry very much when a battle opened badly. He was trusted by his men, but not loved. Lee fought with a rapier; Grant with a sledgehammer. But they both had courage, an iron will, inability to acknowledge defeat. They were both gentlemen, trained at West Point, living up to the best traditions of the Army.

It was Grant's inability to admit defeat that spelled trouble for Lee. For when Lee had whipped McClellan and Pope and Burnside and Hooker, they had accepted the verdict of battle and retreated. It was as if they waged war according to the rules, and when they lost the game they left the field. But Grant didn't wage war that way. He was, as Lee once said regretfully, "not a retreating man."

By the end of April, Lee could see that Grant was ready to

100

strike. Where should he make his stand? Where better than
the Wilderness where he had tangled up poor Hooker — the
Wilderness whose scrub oak and pine and underbrush offered
perfect ground for defense.

The Wilderness campaign — really one long battle — lasted
from early May to early June, and saw the most ferocious
fighting of the whole war. Imagine a diagonal line of about
sixty miles stretching southward from the Rapidan River to
Cold Harbor, just a few miles from Richmond. Like all his
predecessors, Grant was aiming at Richmond. To get there
he had either to break through Lee's lines or slip around them
and get in behind. Lee's job was to tangle him up in the Wilderness, beat back his attacks, edge him constantly away from
Richmond. The fighting took place all along that sixty-mile
line. Grant would smash at Lee and be hurled back; then he
would pull himself together and, instead of retreating, file away
to the south and attack again. Lee had never met an opponent
like that. Attack, repulse, slide; attack, repulse, slide — that
was pretty much the story.

All month long it went on, the soldiers in their heavy woolen
uniforms, carrying fifty pounds of arms and equipment, fighting
by day and marching and digging in by night. With 60,000
men Lee stood and beat off the attacks of an army of twice that
size. There was a whole series of savage battles — Spottsylvania,

the Bloody Angle, The North Anna, Hanover Court House, Cold Harbor. Each time Grant struck, Lee figured out where the blow was coming, and got his army in position, the men cutting down trees and underbrush for defense, digging themselves in, and awaiting the attack. Each time the Federals thrust into the butternut lines they were driven back.

Once Grant made a real break-through that threatened to split Lee's army in two. It was at Spottsylvania Court House. The Federals discovered a weak spot in Lee's line and just at dawn came pouring in by the thousands. Lee, who had been up most of the night, dashed to the front.

"Hold on," he cried to his men. "We are going to form a new line."

General Gordon hurried up and prepared to counter-attack with two fresh brigades. Just in time Gordon realized that Lee, his fighting blood up, was planning to lead the attack himself.

"Go back, General," he cried, "we will drive them back. These men are Virginians and Georgians. They have never failed. They never will. Will you, boys?"

"No," they shouted, and then, "General Lee to the rear, Lee to the rear!" "Go back, General Lee, we can't charge until you go back."

As Lee hesitated, Gordon reached over, took Traveller's

102

bridle, and turned horse and rider in the other direction. Gordon's men attacked with superb courage, but the Federals, too, threw in re-enforcements. Lee hurried off for help, and when he found a new force, turned Traveller once again towards the enemy and rode into the rain of shells coming from the Union ranks. For the second time that morning the cry arose, "Go back, General. for God's sake, go back."

"If you will promise me to drive those people from our works, I will go back," said Lee. The soldiers shouted their promise — and went in and kept it.

Balked again and again by Lee's heroic defense, Grant refused to quit. Every day his casualty list got longer and longer until a cry went up in the North to remove "Butcher Grant." But Lincoln said, "I cannot spare this man. He fights." By the end of May, Grant had lost 50,000 men, and he was no nearer to capturing Richmond than when he started. He made one last desperate effort to break Lee's iron lines. At Cold Harbor, on the edge of the historic Chickahominy, he hurled most of his army in charge after charge. From five in the morning to high noon the Federals came on, wave after wave surging up to the edge of the Confederate trenches, and then ebbing back. That morning cost Grant ten thousand men, and gained nothing at all. It was the end of the Wilderness campaign.

Outnumbered two to one, his own men without sufficient arms or ammunition and almost without food, General Lee had defeated the best commander in the Union armies. He had met the largest and best equipped army that had ever been raised in America, and inflicted on it losses equal to the total numbers of his own army — sixty thousand. Yet this victory differed from all previous victories that Lee had won. For though Grant was defeated, he stayed in the field, and kept right on going. After Cold Harbor he gave up the attempt to smash through Lee's lines. But he didn't give up the attempt to reach Richmond. Instead, he used his control of the sea to shift his whole army across the wide James River, and started to move on Richmond from the south.

With that the war entered its last phase. Grant's army settled down at Petersburg, twenty miles from Richmond, and prepared to wear down Lee by sheer weight of numbers. Every day, now, the Confederacy grew weaker. Sherman took Atlanta and began his famous march to the sea. Thomas conquered Tennessee and destroyed Hood's army at the two battles of Franklin and Nashville. Soon Phil Sheridan, greatest of Union cavalry leaders, swept down the Valley of Virginia, the granary of the South, burning and pillaging, leaving it so bare that he boasted a crow would have to carry his own rations as he flew over it. As for Lee, his army was melting away — by desertion, disease, and death.

"The struggle is to keep the army fed and clothed," he wrote. "Only fifteen in one regiment had shoes, and bacon is issued only once in a few days."

And another time he reported that "the troops were exposed in the line of battle two days, and had been without meat for three days, and in scant clothing took the cold hail and sleet. The physical strength of the men, if their courage survives, must fail under this treatment."

Their courage did survive, but their strength failed. "I fear,"

106

Lee said sadly to President Davis, "a great calamity will befall us."

That spring of 1865, the calamity fell. Grant's army, re-enforced by sea, grew steadily larger. With fresh troops he was able to push his lines farther and farther south, in an effort to swing around Lee. The starving, exhausted Army of Northern Virginia, reduced now to a mere 40,000, was stretched to the breaking point. In February, 1865, appeared a new danger. Sherman had completed his march to the sea, taken Savannah, turned north and was sweeping through the Carolinas headed for Virginia. Within a few weeks he would be able to join

107

hands with Grant. Then Lee would face an army three or four times his size. Unwilling to retreat without a fight, Lee made one last desperate attempt to break Grant's lines. He failed. Then he told President Davis that he would have to retreat. That meant giving up Richmond — Richmond which he had defended so heroically for three bitter years.

April second the retreat began, the long columns in butternut homespun looking like an army of scarecrows. Racing along the valley of the little Appomattox River, it headed for the West. Lee was trying to reach the mountains, where he hoped that he could join the remnants of Johnston's army from North Carolina and continue the fight.

His chances were slender, for Grant was snapping at his heels. Yet he might have made it, had it not been that through some terrible blunder there were no supplies for his famished men at Amelia Court House. He had to stop and forage for food, and even as he was held there, Phil Sheridan's cavalry swept down on his front, cutting off further retreat.

It was the end. What should Lee do? Two courses were open. He could disperse his army, every man for himself, make good his own escape, and try to rally a new army and fight a guerrilla war in the mountains and valleys of the West. Or he could surrender. As for surrender, "I would rather die a thousand deaths," he said. But what course was best for his soldiers, for his people, for his country? What course was right? Clearly it would be wrong to condemn his people to years of guerrilla warfare. He allowed no considerations of vanity, or of his own wishes to color his judgment. To an officer who asked him what history would say of surrender, he answered in words that sum up his whole character:

> I know they will say hard things of us; they will not understand how we were overwhelmed by numbers. But that is not the question, Colonel. The question is — Is it *right* to surrender this army? If it is right, then I will take all the responsibility.

108

And so, with heavy heart, he wrote Grant that he would discuss the terms of surrender. The two met at a little red brick house in the village of Appomattox Court House. Lee rode on Traveller. He had changed from the worn uniform which for months had served him in the field to the only other clothes he had: a splendid full-dress uniform, with a broad sash around his belt, his boots shining like a mirror, his gleaming sword in a magnificent scabbard. Grant was in the uniform of a private, a dusty blouse, trousers spattered with mud, tucked inside his boots, no sword or spurs, nothing to show that he was commander-in-chief except his shoulder straps with their golden stars.

But the rough-appearing Union commander was a gentleman. He did not ask for Lee's sword. His terms were generous. He sent his own army's rations over to the starving Confederates, and ordered the soldiers to refrain from cheering or firing volleys in celebration of the victory. "The war is over," he said. "The rebels are again our countrymen, and the best way of showing our rejoicing will be to abstain from all such demonstration."

Three days later came the formal surrender. It is described by a Union officer who witnessed it:

> Our earnest eyes scan the busy groups on the opposite slopes, breaking camp for the last time, taking down their little shelter tents and folding them carefully as precious things, then slowly forming ranks as for unwelcome duty. And now they move. The dusky swarms forge forward into gray columns of march. On they come, with the old swinging route step and swaying battle-flags. In the van the proud Confederate ensign — the great field of white with canton of star-strewn cross of blue on a field of red, the regimental battle-flags with the same escutcheon following on, crowded so thick, by thinning out of men, that the whole column seemed crowned with red. . . .
>
> Instructions had been given; and when the head of each division column comes opposite our group, our bugle sounds the signal, and instantly our whole line from right to left, regiment by regiment, gives the soldier's salutation, from the "order

arms" to the old "carry" — the marching salute. Gordon at
the head of the column, riding with heavy spirit and downcast
face, catches the sound of shifting arms, looks up, and taking the
meaning, wheels superbly, making with himself and his horse
one uplifted figure, with profound salutation as he drops the
point of his sword to the boot toe; then facing to his own
command, gives word for his successive brigades to pass us
with the same position of the manual — honor answering honor.
On our part not a sound of trumpet more, nor roll of drum;
not a cheer, nor word nor whisper of vain-glorying, but an awed
stillness rather, and breath-holding, as if it were the passing of
the dead.

So ended the Army of Northern Virginia — Lee's army.

He had taken it when it was beaten and disorganized, he had named it, he had welded it into the greatest fighting force of any army in our history, he had led it to victory after futile victory. Now he bade it farewell:

> After four years of arduous service, marked by unsurpassed courage and fortitude, the Army of Northern Virginia has been compelled to yield to overwhelming numbers and resources. I need not tell the survivors of so many hard-fought battles, who have remained steadfast to the last, that I have consented to this result from no distrust of them; but, feeling that valour and devotion could accomplish nothing that could compensate for the loss that would have attended the continuation of the contest, I have determined to avoid the useless sacrifice of those whose past services have endeared them to their countrymen. ... You will take with you the satisfaction that proceeds from the consciousness of duty faithfully performed; and I earnestly pray that a merciful God will extend to you His blessing and protection. With an increasing admiration of your constancy and devotion to your country, and a grateful remembrance of your kind and generous consideration of myself, I bid you an affectionate farewell.

As he sat astride Traveller his men crowded around him, many with tears streaming down their cheeks, not cheering, but saluting the leader who had never failed them. Then he turned, and rode off into history.